Painful Poetry

Jess Burnette

BookLeaf
Publishing

India | USA | UK

Presentation by *BookLeaf Publishing*

Web: www.bookleafpub.com

E-mail: info@bookleafpub.com

ISBN: 9789363308589

First edition 2024

To Lydia with all my love

<3

ACKNOWLEDGEMENT

I have to thank myself for not giving up even though I've wanted to more times than I can count.

PREFACE

I decided to write this collection in an effort to release and heal. I hope in my own journey to healing I can help others feel understood.

Fake

I smile
because that's what people expect,
because that's what people want.

I smile,
but deep down
I feel like an imposter.

In Pieces

Heartache
creates a divide in your timeline,
when your heart was still whole,
and when it was shattered.

Blank

You were to hold my hand,
to lead the way.

But you gave me to the world
with no skills.
But even worse,
no encouragement,
no advice.

You don't even ask how I've been.
Why I still call is the biggest blank.

Time Warp

How can a day
be an eternity,
yet 20 years
is just gone?

PTSD

Footsteps!

Louder

Faster

Closer

Here

FEAR

Conditional Love

Growing up,
for you I fought.

You had my back,
at least I thought.

such a shame to learn,
your love is bought.

The Mystery

How
do you live in my thoughts
when I never
cross yours?

How does one turn off

care?
worry?
love?

without becoming cold?

Thoughtless

Oh but I think SO much,
too much.
So much that
ALL I DO is think.

Well aware of my problems,
yet feel so out of control.
I've wanted to do better,
I've tried to BE better.

Year after year
of disappointment,
and I'm just
so
tired
of
trying.

Unfound

9

Still I wait,
I long to see,
someone who looks,
somewhat like me.

Who are they
if they're out there?
Do they know of me?
Do they care?

Boyfriend

What you call love
is a twisted lust.
You don't care for me,
only stare at my bust.

You say you love me,
but do you really?
I'm simultaneously feeling
gross and silly.

Dissociate

You look at me as if
I should have something to say.
While my body's here with you,
my mind is far away.

It's not something I wish,
I should have something to say.
While my body's here with you,
My mind is

far

away.

Therapy

I have to pay you to listen,
to pretend like you care,
simply because
no one really does.

Driven by Sadness

I drew myself in the background;
I felt that was my place.

Born to be a burden,
it's no wonder why
depression has taken the keys.

Pride

Sure,
I'm proud of me.

But I would rather
be proud of myself
for something other than

just

still being here.

Wounds

Deepest
darkest
depths
do
debilitating
damage.

Brother

Even though
we were cut from the same cloth,
we are vastly different.

But we are alike,
in that we are both
broken.

Jaded

The desire is there
To be mad.

I could be
and
I should be.

But a consuming sadness
leaves no room
for anger.

Jaded is what's left.

Release

Holding on is painful,
letting go is hard...

But I have to believe
that embracing life
ever so tight,
will be its own reward.

Aging

A gray hair,
A pain,
A wrinkle,
A nap.

Growing old is
No mishap.

www.ingramcontent.com/pod-product-compliance
Lightning Source LLC
La Vergne TN
LVHW010856200726

843508LV00012B/2916